BAYONET BATTLE TRAINING

A Realistic and Practical Series of Exercises on the Use of the Training Stick and Dummy

by

C. J. TWINE

The Naval & Military Press Ltd

© 2008

CONTENTS

INTRODUCTION

THE orthodox positions and movements of bayonet fighting are so well known in these days that it is quite unnecessary to set them out in detail herein. Indeed, so well known are they in some quarters and so frequently practised, over and over again as a drill, that bayonet fighting has lost all of its thrill and most of its practical fighting value. It must be fully appreciated from the onset that the standard movements are nothing more than the letters in the alphabet of the bayonet and that the ability to repeat them, one after another, is not proof of actual fighting efficiency, even as the ability to recite the letters of the alphabet does not prove that one is able to group these letters into words or the words into sentences. Much more is demanded of the exponent of the bayonet than the aptitude to perform the standard movements, however smartly or correctly they may be executed.

Once the movements are known and despite the many minor faults that are observable the student of the bayonet must learn to combine them into one continuous movement of aggressive defence and attack: he must learn to group them into a combat. He must acquire, through practical experience, a knowledge of the methods of following up should any of his moves be countered, how to make openings in the guard of his opponent by the use of the feint. He must develop a high standard of co-ordination between mind and muscular action and a fine sense of control, a quick eye and an ever-aggressive spirit.

Can all these most desirable qualities be developed whilst at work against a static target such as a hanging or a prone dummy sack; can a quick eye or the ability to follow up, agility, aggression, initiative be developed by the continual practice of bayonet movements with nothing more formidable than the thin air as an opponent? If real fighting efficiency is to be developed one fact is vital—we must train as we expect and intend to fight; the conditions of our training must be as near to those of actual combat as is practicable. We must train to use the standard movements and any others we may be able to work out against an opponent who is able to think and act even as we can ourselves: he must be able to hit back at us, to dodge and feint, to thrust and counter, and to demand of us not only the ability to perform physically but mentally too. In our practice there must be a vital sense of personal competition, a stimulating sense of skill and achievement.

The introduction of these essential factors into the training must be the objective of our endeavour and is the reason for this book.

THE ESSENTIALS
OF SUCCESSFUL TRAINING

KNOWING the objective of our training to be the development of real fighting efficiency and having decided that actual combat is the only path by which we can attain it, upon what principles are we to base our training? What essential points must we observe if this objective is to be gained?

We have to advance from the stage of performing single movements and develop the capacity to participate successfully in actual competitive combat. Advancement, then, is the first essential of the training. During each training period some definite progress must be made and each period must demand more skill and efficiency than the last, each lesson or practice must convince the pupil that he has made some observable progress, however small it may be. Nothing is more degrading to a keen sense of interest or more demoralizing than continual training without progress or advancement. It is imperative, therefore, that all training and each training period, be it ten minutes or an hour in duration, should be carefully designed to give some advancement.

Continuity of training periods is our second essential, frequent and short periods being preferable to long practices at intermittent intervals. Bayonet training, especially as set out herein, is strenuous and demands the expenditure of much energy; consequently, practices of too long duration will cause muscle tiredness with a resultant loss of interest and efficiency. If the periods are at long intervals that easy familiarity of the movements will not be retained and much of the training value will be lost. Our rule and second essential must be " Frequent short practices make perfect."

It must be remembered that we all differ considerably in bodily structure, in height, weight, length of limb, and in our ability to co-ordinate mind and muscle, and it would be foolish, in consequence, to endeavour to standardize our methods of action or our stance. Every one of us will have his own natural method of action and, provided that it does not have any serious detrimental effect upon our fighting potential, it should be encouraged and developed. It is obviously preferable to fight in our own natural style and to get our man than to endeavour to use some style which, although foreign to us, we have been told we should use and lose speed and probably the combat into the bargain. Use your own style, eliminate its faults and develop its advantages; above all, be comfortable in action. Our third essential, then, is to develop a free and natural style.

5

Balance, control, speed of action and the ability to follow up one movement with another are all so dependent upon good footwork that the development of a correct economy of foot movement must be looked upon as one of the essentials of successful training. It is obvious that in the heat of mortal combat we can hardly expect to think about the movements of our feet; if we wish to benefit by the advantages offered by good footwork we must aim to develop it as a habit so that we shall use the most advantageous foot movements automatically and without thought whenever we go into action with our bayonet. This necessitates continual practice of combined foot and bayonet movements, and to assist the development of this valuable combination some foot movements have been suggested and will be found in the explanations of the various exercises herein. If the movements set out do not suit you, however, work out your own; there is no rule about it, and as long as you are able to perform with speed and decision it is certain that the movements that you use are correct for you, if not for others.

To summarize, then, we have four major factors to bear in mind throughout the training:

(a) Progression of training.

(b) Continuity of training periods

(c) Development of our own natural style of action.

(d) Observance of good foot movements and the synchronization of them with the body and bayonet movements.

THE BAYONET TRAINING STICK

ITS CONSTRUCTION AND USE

THE training stick is simply a one-inch-diameter rod about six feet long with a three-inch-diameter padded knob at one end and a three to four-inch-diameter metal or wire ring at the other end. Fig. 1 illustrates a simple and strong method of construction. The correct use of this apparatus offers a practical and highly interesting method of producing actual combat conditions and helps to develop those qualities which are so essential to the exponent of the bayonet.

In use the stick represents the rifle and bayonet of the instructor, the knob end being the point of his bayonet and the ring end a target or a vulnerable spot on his body. With the knob end the instructor makes thrusts or " points " at the pupil,

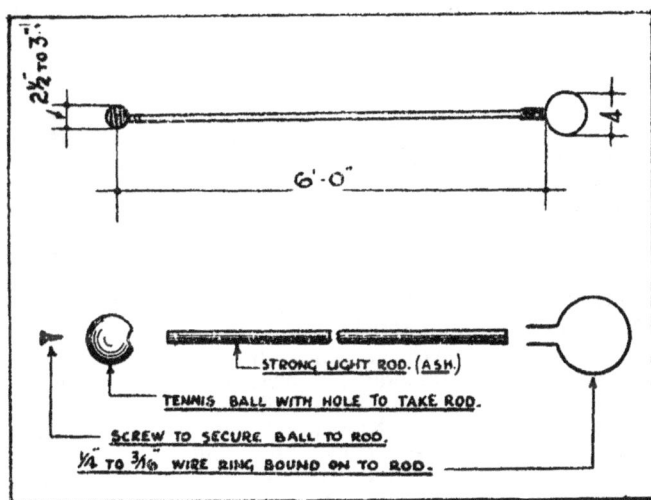

2½" TO 3"

6'·0"

4"

STRONG LIGHT ROD. (ASH.)

TENNIS BALL WITH HOLE TO TAKE ROD.

SCREW TO SECURE BALL TO ROD.

¼ TO ³⁄₁₆ WIRE RING BOUND ON TO ROD.

Fig. 1.—*Construction of the Training Stick.*

who parries them, whilst the pupil points at the ring end of the stick, as if it were the body of his opponent, whenever and wherever the instructor presents it.

The·most practical method of training with the stick is to commence by practice, in slow time and from a standing position, of single points and parries, butt strokes and defences against butt strokes, short points and slashes; and as these movements are mastered gradually combine them, step by step, into sets or sequences of movements, and as confidence and skill develop they can be performed faster and faster. For example, let us first practise just a right parry, later a single point, then combine the two and perform them as one movement, slowly at first and gradually developing speed. Now we can practise a double point and then add this to our last movement, forming a parry, a point and then a double point. Thus we can build up from single movements to continuous combat.

It is wise, in the early stages of training, that both the pupil and instructor should know exactly what movement is to be practised and that the instructor should not attempt to trick the pupil in any way. As progress is made, the training can develop

7

into spontaneous combat and the instructor can use any trick or feint that may occur to him. In this way the training will become most exciting and exhilarating, and will develop in the pupil a very real and practical fighting ability with the bayonet.

A series of progressive instructions on exercises and movements with the training stick is set out herein for your guidance, but, remember, if bayonet fighting is to be successful it must not be limited in its methods nor tied down by any rigid rules or standard movements. Do not be satisfied with the movements found herein, for satisfaction destroys advancement and leads to stagnation. Work out for yourself other movements, anything that may occur to you, however unorthodox they may be. Initiative and imagination must be given every consideration if the training is to be really successful.

The rudimentary movements and positions which precede each engagement with the training stick must first be clearly understood, as they are important from a disciplinary point of view besides lending speed and interest to the work. At the beginning of each bout the pupil will stand, with his rifle and bayonet, in the " rest " position before the instructor (*i.e.*, he stands, left foot advanced and with the butt of his rifle resting on the ground between his feet) and at least some three to four yards away. It is important that the scabbard, complete with belt frog, should be covering the bayonet and that the loop of the frog should be over the hilt of the bayonet, or the scabbard can be secured with a piece of string, to ensure that it does not pull off and an accident occur.

The instructor stands facing the pupil holding the training stick as if it were a rifle and bayonet, with the knob end advanced and resting on the ground. The ring end will be up under his right elbow (see Fig. 2). Whilst the instructor stands thus with the knob resting on the ground the pupil will remain in the " rest " position, but as soon as the knob is raised and the instructor comes up " on guard " (see Fig. 3) the pupil will cant his rifle forward and come " on guard." He will now advance to meet the instructor and, in the early stages of training, stop when his bayonet point is just clear of the knob of the stick. They are now ready for action.

One point is worthy of note at this juncture: the pupil always advances towards the instructor and never the instructor towards the pupil. If in his eagerness the pupil should advance too near and the bayonet point comes nearer to the instructor than the knob end of the stick the instructor will retreat until the bayonet point is clear of the knob by an inch or two.

There are two very sound reasons for this preliminary manœuvre. Firstly, the movements cannot be performed cor-

Fig. 2.—*At " Rest" with the Training Stick.*

Fig. 3.—*" On Guard " or " Ready" with the Training Stick.*

rectly if the bayonet and training stick are crossed prior to action, and, secondly, as the bayonet fighter never retreats when in action this complex of aggression must be developed by the pupil whilst he is in training. The pupil must push the fight and attack always.

When the instructor is training a squad it is a good plan to arrange the pupils in a large circle round the instructor. All will stand in the "rest" position and as soon as the knob is raised and pointed at any one particular pupil he will come "on guard" and advance towards the instructor. When the bout is completed the knob will be lowered to the ground and the pupil will return to the circle. The instructor now swings about and repeats the performance with another pupil.

By the use of this method each pupil will get his practice and as he is unaware of when it may occur he must constantly remain on the alert. All will get their rest periods and, whilst at rest, will be the interested spectators of the combat in progress in the circle. In this way, even when not actually at work with the instructor, each pupil can be learning and at the very least the vital interest of the class will be maintained throughout the practice period.

Throughout the following descriptions of the bayonet and training stick movements it has been assumed that the preliminary sparring has been completed and that the instructor has given the pupil the "on guard" by raising the knob of the training stick from the ground, and they stand facing ready for action. Movements or exercises headed by such remarks, in brackets, as "(to the right)" or "(to the left)" indicate the direction of movement from the pupil's point of view, whilst directional notes for the instructor will be given from his own viewpoint. For example, if an exercise is headed "Long point (to the left)" the pupil will, in this exercise, make a point to his own left front, whilst the instructor's directions in this case will be "Present the ring to your right side." The left of the instructor will be the right of the pupil and vice versa—a point that must be remembered.

We shall be concerned with two main methods of delivering "points" from the standing or advancing position; firstly, a "point" from the "on guard" position without any foot movement and, secondly, a "point," of much longer range, made by advancing the right foot a good long pace simultaneously with the bayonet thrust. The latter of these methods is generally the most advantageous in actual use because it gives longer killing range to the bayonet and enables a point to be made from a less vulnerable position, also the body is well balanced after the thrust has been made and consequently it is possible to follow up the first movement quickly with another. Both methods

10

should be practised with the training stick, however, as it is wise to be competent in the use of both.

Firstly, let us deal with the practice of points:—

Exercise No. 1

POINT (TO THE LEFT) WITHOUT FOOT MOVEMENT

(a) **Instructor** withdraws the knob of the stick with his left hand to his left side and presents the ring with his right hand to his right side about waist- or chest-high (see Fig. 4).

(b) **Pupil** makes his point through the ring, without any foot movement, withdraws, comes up " on guard " and advances past the instructor, right shoulder to right shoulder. He then turns about and faces the instructor, still " on guard."

(c) **Instructor** turns about as pupil advances and comes back " on guard " if he wishes the pupil to advance again and continue the action or, if he wants to conclude it, places the knob on the ground.

Fig. 4.—*Instructor presents Ring for Point to Left (as viewed by pupil).*

Exercise No. 2

POINT (TO THE RIGHT) WITHOUT FOOT MOVEMENT

(a) **Instructor,** whilst withdrawing the knob and presenting the ring as in Exercise No. 1, pivots left about on his left foot, thus presenting the ring on the opposite side (see Fig. 5).

(b) **Pupil** will make his " point " without foot movement, withdraw from the ring and advance past the instructor, " on guard," left shoulder to left shoulder. He now turns about and awaits further instructions.

(c) **Instructor,** being already turned about, now faces the pupil again; he then comes " on guard " or " rests " as he wishes.

It may be found that in Exercises Nos. 1 and 2 the pupil is unable to pass his bayonet through the ring because it is too far away. This illustrates clearly the need for a " point " of longer range, which will be dealt with in Exercises Nos. 3 and 4.

FIG. 5.—*Instructor presents Ring for Point to Right (as viewed by pupil).*

Exercise No. 3

POINT WITH FOOT MOVEMENT (TO THE LEFT)

(a) **Instructor** will move as in Exercise No. 1, presenting the ring on his right side (see Fig. 4). In addition, he will take a pace backwards to lengthen the range for the pupil.

(b) **Pupil** will make point advancing with his right foot as he thrusts; he then withdraws, without moving his feet, comes up " on guard " and, advancing his left foot, at the same time passes the instructor right shoulder to right shoulder. He now turns about as before.

(c) **Instructor** turns about as in Exercise No. 1.

Fig. 6.—*Instructor makes a " Point " with Training Stick.*

Exercise No. 4

POINT WITH FOOT MOVEMENT (TO THE RIGHT)

(a) **Instructor** will move as for Exercise No. 2, presenting the ring on the opposite side (see Fig. 5), but will, in addition, move a pace away from the pupil.

(b) **Pupil** makes his point to the right front advancing the right foot, withdraws without foot movement and comes " on guard " as his first left pace past the instructor is taken. He turns about as before.

(c) **Instructor** is already turned about, so he comes " on guard " or " rests."

These movements should be practised slowly at first until the fundamental positions have been mastered, then they can be gradually speeded up and the instructor can present the ring, be it to right or left, at different heights, or in varying positions (see dotted lines in Figs. 4 and 5). The pupil should endeavour

13

throughout to pass only the first three or four inches of his bayonet through the ring and to withdraw quickly and cleanly.

Now we can advance a stage farther and practise our parries. The movements of the instructor will offer the most interest to you, as, no doubt, the pupil's movements for the orthodox right and left parries are well known by you.

When thrusting in the stick, knob first, so that the pupil can parry it, the instructor releases his hold upon it with his left hand as the movement is made, and thrusts it in towards the pupil with his right hand (see Fig. 6).

No attempt should be made to actually hit the pupil, and as the stick is parried to one side it should drop so that the knob is on the ground; then the left hand can again grasp the stick ready for any further action. If the pupil is to practise a left parry the instructor must send in the stick on *his* right side of the bayonet, or if a right parry is to be executed then the stick will be thrust in on the instructor's left side of the bayonet. Practise a few parries to the right and left, and aim to develop in the pupil the ability to parry cleanly with the least amount of sideways movement of the rifle and bayonet. Even when practising a single parry with the aid of the training stick advance past the instructor as described in Exercise No. 1, as it will help to develop speed and initiative.

When the parries have been practised we can advance to a more interesting stage of our training and take the first major step towards our objective—fighting efficiency—by learning to combine parries and points. It must always be appreciated that our method of bayonet fighting must be one of continual aggressive and ruthless attack, and consequently we must learn to look upon such movements as parries not as defensive movements but as constructive feints and movements which must be exploited by us as a chance of counter-attack.

By combining the few exercises already covered we can develop, even at this early stage of training, quite a large variety of sets or sequences of movements and the work can become very interesting. The pupil can practise a parry to the left followed up by a point to the left; the point can be a short- or long-range movement as described in Exercises Nos. 1 or 3. A parry to the right and long- or short-range point to the right, a left parry and point to the right or a right parry and point to the left can now be practised, and with such a repertoire at our command there is no reason why we should not participate in a certain amount of quite spontaneous action. For example, we face our instructor at the " on guard " and we have no idea of the movement we are to perform. Suddenly, without any warning, he thrusts in the knob end of the stick on the left side (instructor's right side) of our bayonet. This calls for a left parry, which we perform. As soon as we have made our parry the instructor steps backwards quickly and presents the ring on our right front (his left side) and we follow up with a good long point through the ring, withdraw and pass through at the " on guard." We turn about to find the instructor still " on guard," so we advance again and he suddenly presents the ring on our left front (his right side). In we go with our point, withdraw and pass through to find that the knob has been placed on the ground, so we place our rifle butt on the ground and take a well-earned rest.

From the actions already mentioned there arise two important factors which must be given careful consideration. The first is that whilst we are performing a right parry we are vulnerable to a butt stroke from our opponent and, secondly, when we are performing a left parry we could use a butt stroke ourselves to no mean advantage. We do not wish to open our guard and enable our opponent to use a butt stroke, yet we must use our right parry. It is obvious, then, that we must have a defence ready and this defence must form a starting-point for an aggressive attack from us; also we would like to make use of the opening that we see in our opponent's guard when we parry his bayonet to our left. Exercises Nos. 5 and 6 will be found to give practical answers to both these items.

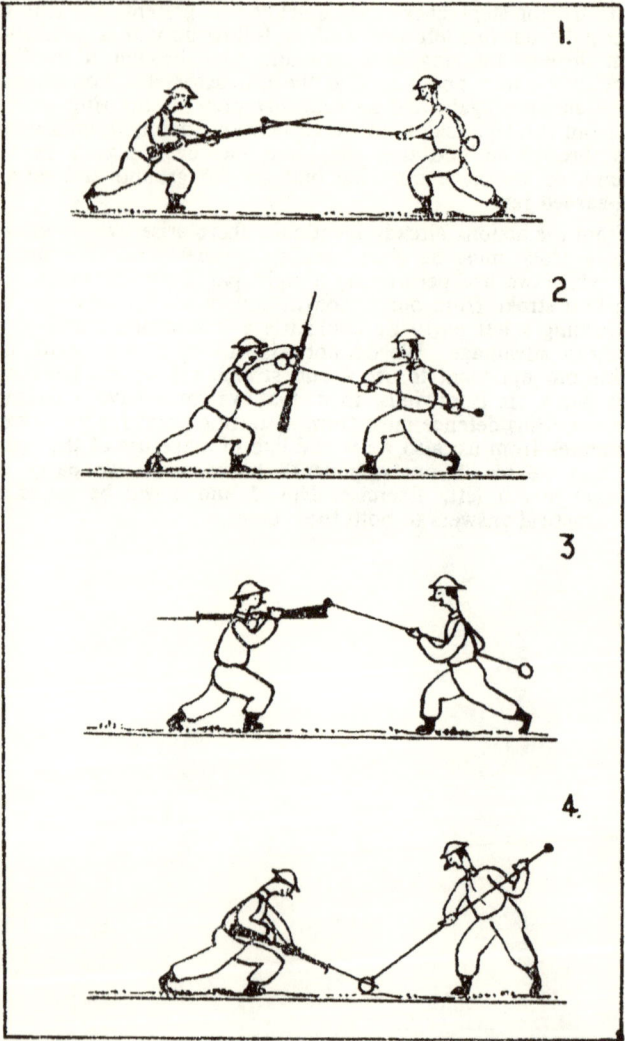

FIG. 7.

16

Exercise No. 5

RIGHT PARRY—DEFENCE AGAINST BUTT STROKE— HEEL JAB—POINT TO KILL

(a) **Instructor** thrusts in knob end of stick to left (*i.e.*, pupil's right side), retaining in this case his left-hand grasp on the stick (Fig. 7, 1).

(b) **Pupil** makes a right parry (Fig. 7, 1).

(c) **Instructor,** as pupil parries, swings the ring end round, right to left, towards side of pupil's head (Fig. 7, 2).

(d) **Pupil** raises left hand until rifle and bayonet are held in a vertical position in front of the body, left hand about as high as the top of his head, and holding it in this way swings it from right to left so that the ring is countered and prevented from contacting the head (Fig. 7, 2).

(e) **Instructor** leaps well back as soon as the pupil counters the ring, and places the knob end of the stick in the position occupied by his own head prior to his backward leap (Fig. 7, 3).

(f) **Pupil,** having countered the butt stroke, swings the bayonet over his left shoulder with his left hand and, advancing his right foot, smashes the heel of his rifle butt upwards with his right hand to the knob of the stick (*i.e.*, his opponent's head) (Fig. 7, 3).

(g) **Instructor** now places ring on the ground, representing the pupil's opponent now on the ground (Fig. 7, 4).

(h) **Pupil** follows up his last move and delivers a killing point to the ring, withdraws and advances " on guard " as before (Fig. 7, 4).

All this may appear rather complicated at first sight, but one or two slow practice bouts will soon make the sequence of movements quite clear. It will be apparent, once this exercise has been performed, that good footwork is essential if speed is to be attained. Work out for yourself the foot movements which enable you to execute this exercise with the maximum speed and balance and then set to work to develop them as a habit. The following movements are suggested for your guidance: make the right parry and counter the butt stroke from the orthodox " on guard " position without moving the feet and as you swing up the butt to the head of the opponent advance the right leg a full pace to bring you well within range. Now as the " point " is delivered advance the left foot again, withdraw, and pass through " on guard."

Now to practise the butt stroke as a " follow up " from the left parry.

FIG. 8.

Exercise No. 6

LEFT PARRY—BUTT STROKE—POINT TO KILL

(a) **Instructor** thrusts in the knob end of the stick to his right (*i.e.*, pupil's left), releasing the stick with his left hand (Fig. 8, 1).

(b) **Pupil** makes a left parry, but continues the right to left movement of the bayonet (Fig. 8, 1).

(c) **Instructor** leaps backwards as soon as the pupil has made his left parry, allowing the pupil to make his butt stroke to the knob of the stick which is now in the position occupied by the head of the instructor prior to his leap (Fig. 8, 2).

18

(d) **Pupil** continues as from (b), and, pivoting on the left foot, advances the right and smashes the butt to the knob of the stick (Fig. 8, 2).

(e) **Instructor** now places the ring end of the stick on the ground to his right front, that is, in the position that the opponent of the pupil would have fallen after receiving the butt stroke on the side of his head (Fig. 8, 3).

(f) **Pupil** now follows up his butt stroke with a point to the ring, withdraws, comes up " on guard " again and advances past the instructor, right shoulder to right shoulder (Fig. 8, 3).

Both pupil and instructor will turn about after this movement, as for the other exercises, and continue the combat or rest as the instructor will indicate by the position of the knob of his training stick.

Having practised Exercises Nos. 5 and 6, we can include them in our repertoire of movements for free practice or spontaneous combat and some excellent bouts should now be possible. The instructor, too, will now have to be most vigilant because when he thrusts in the knob, intending to follow up by presenting the ring for a point, he may discover that the pupil, having made a left parry, is developing a butt stroke. The instructor can fall in with the plan or he can retreat quickly, still " on guard " with his stick, and wait for the pupil to close with him again. Alternatively, as the instructor notices that the pupil is about to deliver a butt stroke, he can leap back and present the ring, in any position, for the pupil to " kill," and just when the pupil is about to deliver his point the ring can be withdrawn and in can go the knob at the pupil, who will need all his wits about him to make a parry and follow up. The combat can continue in this way for as long as the instructor wishes, and the battle can rage, backwards and forwards, with first one taking the initiative and then the other wresting it from him, and so on *ad libitum*.

There is one eventuality we must consider and be prepared for when we use a butt stroke as a " follow up " from a left parry. If the opponent is able to duck under our rifle butt as it swings round how can we follow up quickly? Having missed our opponent's head, we use the " back slash " stroke and by swinging our rifle back again, from left to right, smash the heel of the butt to any vulnerable part of the opponent's body. If this blow is successfully delivered we can expect our opponent to fall to our right front, so we must follow up quickly with a killing point.

The movements of pupil and instructor for this action will be found in Exercise No. 7.

FIG. 9.

Exercise No. 7

LEFT PARRY—BUTT STROKE (TO MISS)—BACK SLASH —POINT TO KILL

(a) **Instructor** thrusts in knob to his right front (*i.e.*, pupil's left) (Fig. 9, 1).

(b) **Pupil** parries as in Exercise No. 6 and makes his butt stroke (Fig. 9, 1).

(c) **Instructor** leaps backwards as in Exercise No. 6, and places knob end of the stick in position for pupil's butt stroke, but as the butt is swung round the stick is lowered quickly so as to cause the pupil to miss with his butt. It is then raised again into its former position (Fig. 9, 2).

(d) **Pupil,** having missed the stick with his butt stroke, swings the rifle back, left to right, and delivers a " back slash " stroke, with the heel of the butt, to the stick (Fig. 9, 3).

(e) **Instructor** assumes that the last action has felled the pupil's opponent to his (the instructor's) left side, so he now places the ring end of the stick in this position on the ground (Fig. 9, 4).

(f) **Pupil** now follows up his " back slash " with a point to the ring, withdraws, and passes through " on guard " as before (Fig. 9, 4).

With regard to the last two exercises, the instructor may experience some difficulty in leaping back and presenting the knob as the head of the pupil's opponent. If this is so, it is suggested that, after sending in the stick for the parry, the instructor retreats and allows the pupil to make his butt stroke or back slash at an imaginary target, and whilst he is doing this the instructor places the ring on the ground ready for the pupil to make his final kill.

There may occur, under the conditions of actual combat, circumstances when, having made a killing point at one opponent, we are engaged by a second before we are able to get back " on guard." We must, therefore, prepare and train to meet such attacks by participation in bouts as described in Exercise No. 8.

FIG. 10.

22

Exercise No. 8

DOUBLE POINTS (TO RIGHT OR LEFT)

(a) **Instructor** advances ring (to his right or left) as described in Exercises Nos. 1 and 2 (Fig. 10, 1).

(b) **Pupil** makes his first point (to right or left), advancing his right foot simultaneously (Fig. 10, 1), and withdraws without moving his feet (Fig. 10, 2).

(c) **Instructor** steps backwards about two feet, still presenting the ring (Fig. 10, 2).

(d) **Pupil** makes his second " point " straight from the " withdraw " position of his first movement, advancing his left foot as he thrusts. He now withdraws again, comes up " on guard " and advances as before (Fig. 10, 3).

The descriptions of movements in Exercise No. 8 are simply an example of this type of action and a basis upon which to build any similar action that may occur to you. Once the routine of the " double " action is understood, the instructor can present the ring for the second " point " in a different position, higher or lower, to the right or left, so that the pupil will develop the ability to meet the second attack from any angle.

Having practised the simple " double points," we can advance a stage and combine them with any of the exercises previously described. For example, perform Exercise No. 6 and as the pupil withdraws from his final point the instructor will step back and present the ring again. The pupil will now attack the ring (a second opponent) straight from his last withdrawal and without coming up " on guard." It is a wise plan to practise parries as well as points from the " final withdrawal " position; a second instructor can be introduced and he can thrust in his stick as the pupil withdraws from his last point. The pupil will parry this thrust and attack again, the second instructor this time, with any of the movements he has been learning.

Here is another movement which will give interesting work with the training stick and which can, in due course, be added to our list of movements for the free practice periods.

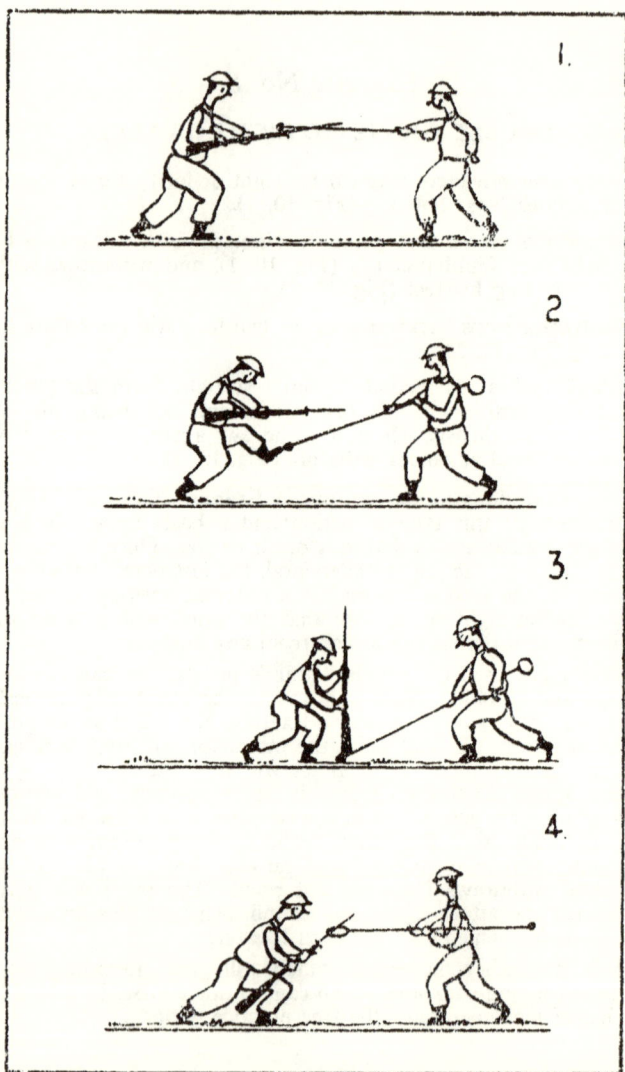

FIG. 11.

24

Exercise No. 9

RIGHT PARRY—KICK TO FORK—BUTT SMASH— SHORT JAB POINT TO SECOND OPPONENT

(a) **Instructor** thrusts in the knob on his left side (*i.e.*, pupil's right side) (Fig. 11, 1).

(b) **Pupil** makes a right parry, advancing right foot a short pace at the same time (Fig. 11, 1).

(c) **Instructor** leaps well back as soon as the parry is made, and presents the knob in the position occupied by his own fork or crutch prior to his leap backward (Fig. 11, 2).

(d) **Pupil** now makes a left-foot kick at the knob (Fig. 11, 2).

(e) **Instructor** places ring end of the stick on the ground in front of the pupil to represent the fallen opponent (Fig. 11, 3).

(f) **Pupil** swings his rifle up vertically in front of his body and smashes the heel of the butt downwards to hit the ground just by the ring (Fig. 11, 3). (There is no need to actually hit the ring, as it might be damaged.)

(g) **Instructor** takes a pace back quickly as soon as the butt of the rifle contacts the ground and presents the ring, to his front, about waist- or chest-high, two feet away from the pupil (Fig. 11, 4).

(h) **Pupil**, with his butt still on the ground, moves his right hand up the rifle and places it just below his left hand. From this position he makes a " jab " point upwards through the ring, withdraws, moves his right hand back again, and advances " on guard " as before (Fig. 11, 4).

Again a second instructor can be introduced in this exercise, and his job would be to present the ring, standing well behind the first instructor, for the pupil to make his short " jab " point. Having made his " jab " and withdrawn, the pupil can close with the second instructor and perform another exercise with him. For example, having withdrawn from his " jab," the pupil might execute a left parry—butt stroke (to miss)—back slash—point to kill, as described in Exercise No. 7, thus combining, in one continuous action, Exercises Nos. 6 and 7. If two, or even three or four, instructors work together a " living " assault course can be introduced. The pupil can engage the first instructor and perform, say, Exercise No. 5: Right parry—defence against butt

25

stroke—heel jab—point to kill." He will now advance "on guard" to the second instructor, who stands about ten to fifteen feet behind the first. The pupil's action with this instructor may be a point to the right followed by a second point to a flank. On he goes again and performs, with the third instructor, some other exercise. As the first pupil passes the first instructor and advances towards the next, a second pupil can begin his assault down the line of instructors and in this way keep a whole squad engaged.

At this stage of the training ground patches can be introduced. Six-inch squares of white card or stiff paper are all that is required, and they are placed on the ground by, or between, the instructors. Their purpose is to serve as additional targets for the pupil's bayonet and can be used, for example, in this way:

A target or ground patch is placed on the ground about two feet away and behind the instructor. The pupil advances and performs a left parry—butt stroke—point to kill with the instructor and his training stick. Straight from his last "withdraw" the pupil will make a long point at the ground patch, withdraw, and pass on again to meet the next instructor. Again, two of these patches could be placed on the ground, about five to six feet apart, and be positioned midway between two instructors. This arrangement would enable the pupil to execute a "double point" as described in Exercise No. 8. Dummy sacks could, of course, be used in place of ground patches, but they are not so portable or so easily made and offer no exceptional advantages from the training point of view.

There is only one other movement with which we need be concerned herein and that is a "throw point." Its purpose is to kill an opponent who has turned to run, and it is delivered straight from the right shoulder, holding the rifle, at the small of the butt, with the right hand, and the left hand is removed entirely. The position of the instructor in Fig. 6 is the "throw point" position. This movement must not be used in actual combat if there is any chance of an attack from another enemy, because the performer is exceedingly vulnerable. You may wish to practise it, however, and it will be executed with the training stick in the following way:

The pupil and instructor stand facing in the "on guard" position. The instructor will present the ring to his right side and well away from his body. He now runs backwards and the pupil follows up with his "throw point" to the ring. If the ring is presented to the instructor's left (see Fig. 5), he will be able to run forwards, and as in this exercise there is little advantage in practising the "throw" to both sides you may find that the second method, presenting the ring to the left, is preferable.

Fig. 12.

Here is the sequence of movements for a "throw point" to the right:

Instructor and Pupil stand "on guard" ready for action (Fig. 12, 1).

Instructor presents the ring to his left side and doubles away from the pupil (Fig. 12, 2).

Pupil delivers his "throw point" straight from the right shoulder, releasing his left-hand grip on the rifle (Fig. 12, 3).

THE DUMMY STICK

ITS CONSTRUCTION AND USE

IT has been discovered that when the pupil has advanced to a certain stage of proficiency he is able, in certain exercises, to move so fast that the instructor experiences considerable difficulty in positioning his stick in time. In the case of Exercise No. 6, for instance, if the pupil follows up his left parry with an exceptionally fast butt stroke, as indeed he should, the instructor may not be able to recover the stick after the parry and place it in position for the butt stroke. Now, the pupil must not be handicapped in his development of speed because the instructor has attained his maximum, and it is essential, therefore, that other methods be used to enable the instructor to increase his rate of action. The dummy stick has been designed to surmount this difficulty.

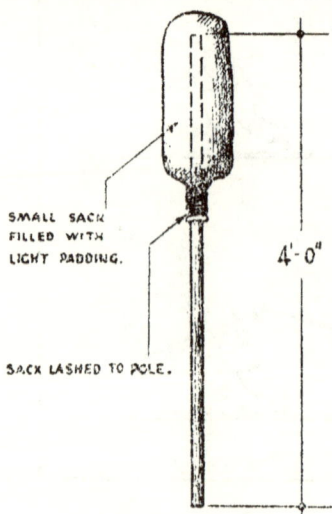

SMALL SACK FILLED WITH LIGHT PADDING.

4'- 0"

SACK LASHED TO POLE.

FIG. 13.

The dummy stick is about four feet long, strong and light, and has fixed to one end of it a small padded sack about twelve inches long and about six to eight inches in diameter. The stick should pass inside the sack and within an inch or two of the bottom (see Fig. 13).

In use the dummy stick will be held by the instructor in one hand and the training stick in the other, and its function in the training will readily be appreciated upon perusal of the following exercises.

*Exercise No. 6*A

LEFT PARRY—BUTT STROKE—POINT TO KILL

(a) **Instructor** holds training stick in his right hand and the dummy stick in his left, with the head end of the dummy level with his own head and about two feet in front of it. He now thrusts in the knob end of the training stick to his right (*i.e.*, pupil's left) (Fig. 14, 1).

(b) **Pupil** parries the stick to his left (Fig. 14, 1).

(c) **Instructor** swings the training stick round behind him as it is parried (Fig. 14, 2).

(d) **Pupil** follows up his left parry and, pivoting on his left foot, advancing his right, and smashes the butt of his rifle to the head of the dummy stick (Fig. 14, 2).

(e) **Instructor** allows the dummy to fall to his right front and places the head on the ground to represent the fallen opponent (Fig. 14, 3).

(f) **Pupil** now makes his killing point at the head of the dummy stick, withdraws and advances " on guard " as before (Fig. 14, 3).

FIG. 14.

FIG. 15.

Exercise No. 7A

LEFT PARRY—BUTT STROKE (TO MISS)—BACK SLASH —POINT TO KILL

(a) **Instructor** stands with training stick in his right hand and dummy stick in his left hand. He thrusts in knob to his right (Fig. 15, 1).

(b) **Pupil** makes his left parry (Fig. 15, 1) and swings round the butt of his rifle to the head of the dummy stick (Fig. 15, 2).

(c) **Instructor** swings training stick behind him as it is parried and quickly lowers the head of the dummy stick to make the pupil miss it with his butt stroke. . He now raises the head again immediately (Fig. 15, 2).

(d) **Pupil**, having missed with his butt stroke, swings his rifle back again, left to right, and slashes the head with the heel of his rifle butt (Fig. 15, 3).

(e) **Instructor** allows head of dummy stick to fall, to his left this time, and places it on the ground ready for the kill (Fig. 15, 4).

(f) **Pupil** follows up his " slash " with a point at the head, withdraws, etc. (Fig. 15, 4).

FIG. 16.

Exercise No. 8A

RIGHT PARRY—KICK TO FORK—BUTT SMASH

(a) **Instructor,** holding the training stick in his left hand and the dummy in his right, head end about two feet from the ground, sends in the knob on his left side (Fig. 16, 1).

(b) **Pupil** makes a right parry, advancing his right foot simultaneously (Fig. 16, 1).

(c) **Instructor** swings the training stick well round to his left as it is parried (Fig. 16, 2).

(d) **Pupil** follows up his right parry with a left-foot kick to head of dummy (*i.e.*, fork of opponent) (Fig. 16, 2).

(e) **Instructor** lowers head of dummy to ground as it is kicked by the pupil (Fig. 16, 3).

(f) **Pupil** follows up his kick with a butt smash to the head (Fig. 16, 3).

We have now covered enough ground to keep us occupied for quite a while. If we develop all these movements to a high degree of efficiency and are able to perform them with speed and aggression, we have every justification to feel confident in our ability as exponents of the bayonet. One point in concluding this chapter: the training stick is an excellent training apparatus when in the hands of the pupil, and it is a good scheme to allow him to take over the stick now and again.

THE USE OF DUMMY SACKS

IT cannot be claimed that static training apparatus, such as hanging or prone dummy sacks, offers the same degree of practical training value as does the use of the stick. The value of this type of apparatus is severely restricted because it cannot offer to the pupil that all-important factor of actual combat, the contest for mastery. Indeed, such apparatus does not even demand of the pupil an alert mind or a dominant spirit of initiative: he knows that his target cannot move, dodge or feint; he knows that he need not expect any counter-attack and, in consequence, he is not exhorted to give himself body and mind to the work.

Training with dummy sacks is limited to the development of " points " and the appreciation of the true killing range of the bayonet, both of which can, however, be practised and developed to a higher degree by working against the training stick. It must be admitted that under certain conditions, especially from the point of view of an instructor, the use of both hanging and prone dummies can be invaluable. The instructor may wish to work alongside the pupil and not facing him, as is the case when the training stick is being used. The use of a dummy sack will free the instructor and enable him to direct the training from any angle he may wish.

It is suggested that, having learned the basic movements of bayonet work, the beginner should pass on to work with a dummy sack as the first stage of his practical training. Here he will develop the ability to " point " with good range and direction and then move on to work with the training stick. The dummy sack should be looked upon as an apparatus to aid the demonstration of the correct methods of delivering " points " and not as a training aid by which the pupil can develop a high degree of fighting efficiency. Remember always that actual competitive combat is the only true path to fighting ability, and static targets offer no competition and do not demand or develop any of the essential qualities of the bayonet fighter.

The exercises with the dummy sacks set out herein cover the entire range of really useful work with this apparatus.

Exercise No. 1

HANGING DUMMY SACK

The object of this exercise is to develop an appreciation of the range of the bayonet.

Stand facing the dummy with the rifle and bayonet in the " on

guard " position and with the right foot advanced; place the first
two or three inches of the bayonet point in the dummy (see Fig.
17, 1). Now gradually work the feet backwards until the arms
are fully extended and the body is inclined as far forward as
possible without loss of balance (see Fig. 17, 2). Now, without
moving the left foot, push back with the right and come up into
the " on guard " position (Fig. 17, 3). Make a mark on the
ground by the toe of the left boot (see arrow " B " in Fig. 17),
and straight from this position make a " point " at the dummy,
advancing the right foot simultaneously. This should bring you
back again into position No. 2 in Fig. 17. Repeat this several
times and check up on the bayonet, making sure that it is only

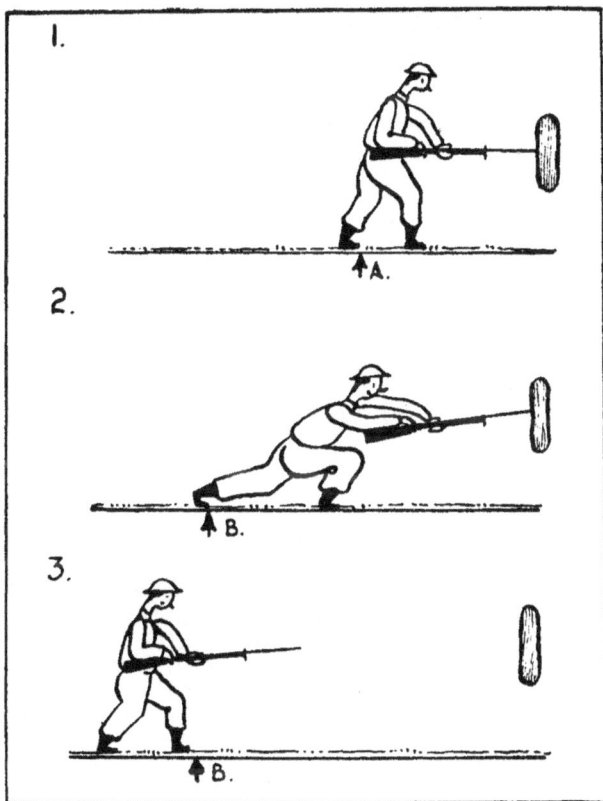

FIG. 17.

35

entering the dummy about two or three inches. Having marked the position of our left foot prior to our " point," move back about fifteen to twenty feet and advance at a walk " on guard " towards the dummy.

As soon as the left foot comes near the mark make the " point." Repeat, advancing a little faster this time, and make the " point " as before. Continue on these lines until a good " point " can be delivered, advancing at a " charge " and drawing only a few inches of steel. Note the distance from the mark on the ground to the sack; in all probability its greatness will surprise you, and as a comparison and a point of interest repeat Exercise No. 1, but, this time, have the left foot advanced (as for the " on guard " position). It will be found that the range of the bayonet has been decreased by some two to three feet. This is an important lesson. A " point " made by advancing the right foot has longer range, carries more weight behind it, and can be delivered from a less vulnerable position.

Up to this stage of our work we have been " pointing " at the sack in general and not at any particular part of it. In actual combat the point of the bayonet must be directed by the left hand towards any specific part of our opponent quickly and accurately. We must therefore introduce the question of direction into the training by one of two methods. Spots can be painted on the sack and as we advance and " point " as in Exercise No. 1 we can now direct the bayonet at one of the spots, or, perhaps a sounder scheme, the instructor can stand to one side of the dummy and, holding a training stick by the knob end, place the ring end flat on the sack to give a target. The instructor can move the ring into any position he wishes as the pupil advances, and in this way keep the pupil on the alert.

Exercises similar to No. 1 can be performed with a prone dummy sack, their object, range and direction being the same.

Stand facing the dummy, right foot advanced, and draw the few inches of bayonet. Now move back until the full range is obtained; keep the left foot in place and swing back " on guard " (see Fig. 18). Mark the position of the left foot and begin to practise as previously described, increasing the speed of the advance until the " point " is being performed from the " charge." When withdrawing after the " point " (Fig. 18, 2), the left foot can be advanced and placed on the dummy to assist the withdrawal. Again, as progress is made, the sack can be marked or the ring end of a training stick used to give a target for the " point." Do not work for too long with static targets; once the range of the bayonet is appreciated and some idea of direction is developed, get to work with the training stick.

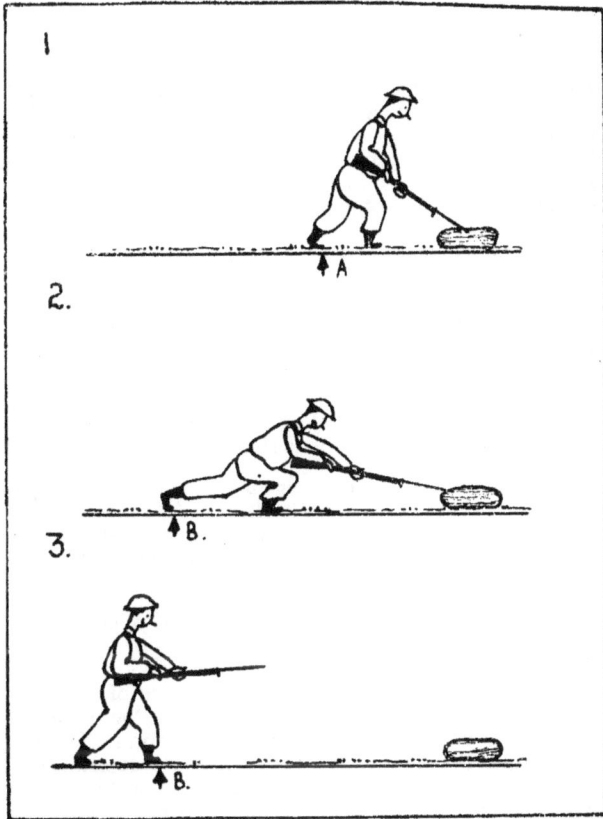

FIG. 18.

37

THE FINAL ASSAULT COURSE

ITS CONSTRUCTION AND USE

WE have been mainly concerned throughout the preceding chapters with the training and development of the bayonet fighter as an individual, and we must not lose sight of the fact that the bayonet is most formidable when used *en masse*. It is most probable that when we go into action with our bayonet we shall operate as one member of a team, as part of the final assault to some tactical manœuvre. Much may depend on the success of the assault: hours of successful scheming and intrigue may be completely nullified and many valuable lives uselessly expended because the final assault has failed to carry its objective. It is imperative, therefore, that we develop our ability to function not only as an individual but as part of a team. Although the technical standard of a team depends upon the personal prowess and skill-at-arms of each member, its success in the field is dependent upon the degree of understanding and support given by each member to his fellows and upon a rigid team code of discipline.

A knowledge of the essential rules of the assault and a willing surrender to its discipline are not sufficient. We must constantly practise and train under these rules and subject to this discipline so that it becomes an inveterate habit and one that is sure to stand the test of mortal combat.

The most vital factor in the final assault of a position, even when supported by the light automatic weapons of to-day, is that the whole party should advance together, in line, each man guarding the flanks of his neighbours. The pace of the advance must be the speed of the slowest member, whilst the more speedy must curb their desire to forge ahead. The moral effect of the bayonet assault, the major factor of success, is dependent upon the simultaneous arrival of the mass at the objective, and any member who arrives, or perhaps more correctly attempts to arrive, ahead of the pack will not only draw the concentrated fire of the enemy upon himself but, what is more important, is exposing the flanks of some of his own men

During an assault one must expect to encounter obstacles, and it is quite probable that the exact nature of these obstacles and their retarding capacity will vary for each man in the assault. Some may find their path fairly clear and straightforward, whilst others will encounter difficulties and their progress will be slowed down; yet the team must arrive at the objective as a team.

38

If our training or practice assault course is to be of real and practical value it must demand, as nearly as possible, the same qualities in the pupil as would an actual assault. There must be the comparatively simple path for some and a more difficult way for others to traverse. Those on a smooth path must learn how to wait for and cover their fellows who have obstacles to surmount. If all have the same set of obstacles to pass, the course has deteriorated into nothing more than a test of the ability to surmount difficulties as an individual and not, as it is intended to be, a training course over which a team can develop the ability to assault in line, and attain their objective as a team, irrespective of the problems and difficulties of the individual.

When about to construct an assault course consider carefully the demands, other than the physical, which would have to be met in actual warfare, and endeavour to design obstacles of " psychological " character, and combine them with the physical type. For example, a pit about ten feet square and three feet deep will present no difficulty whatsoever; any man could traverse it almost without thought, but if the depth of the pit is unknown to the man who has to cross it and he discovers it filled with smoke and the bottom indiscernible, he is immediately faced with a problem the solution of which demands not physical capability but quick thinking and initiative. Endeavour to set mental problems, to demand decisions, to surprise, and develop initiative and resource.

Throughout the training over the course every man should practise firing and reloading from the hip whilst advancing at the double; also each man should carry one or two dummy hand grenades and learn to throw them on the run without exposing himself and his comrades to their dangers.

The tommy-gunner, too, should go over the course and learn to give the fullest support to the bayonet men and yet not expose them to his own fire. When at practice on the range the bomber and the tommy-gunner do not usually operate with their riflemen around them as they would be, in all probability, during an assault. They must get accustomed to their presence or serious casualties may be inflicted by them upon their fellows.

Much interest can be added by the introduction of hanging or prone dummy sacks along the course. They should be arranged, if possible, so that they are concealed from the advancing men until they are right on top of them, thus demanding quick decisions and even quicker actions. The best positions for the dummies are spots which would give cover to an enemy, behind walls, in slit trenches and behind natural cover, for example. These dummies will give an opportunity for a little bayonet work and will add another touch of realism to the training.

The simplest plan is to design the course to accommodate five or six men at a time and to send large numbers over it in details. Naturally it would be preferable to be able to accommodate a whole platoon in one detail, but so large would the course have to be that its construction would become a major undertaking. The course should begin under cover and not, as it so frequently does, in a piece of open ground. When making an assault in actual warfare the assaulting troops approach as near to their objective as is reasonably possible and there, under cover, make their final preparations and position themselves so that on the " advance " the whole force can move forward as one man. So important is this " start " that it justifies some practice, and what more appropriate place can be found for this practice than the assault course?

It is suggested that the first obstacle should be a simple one and should be designed to accommodate every man in the detail. This will tend to steady the assault in its early stages. It is useful, too, to have some dummies behind this obstacle, because the sooner the detail get some action the quicker they will give themselves heart and soul to the job in hand. Fig. 19 illustrates a suitable type of obstacle.

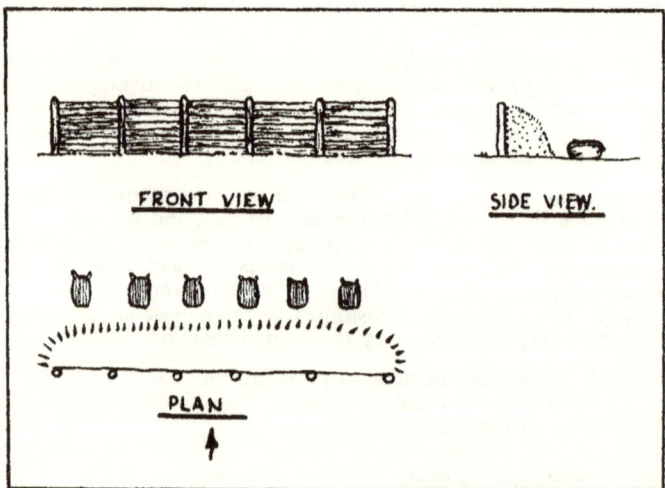

FRONT VIEW   SIDE VIEW.

PLAN

Fig. 19.

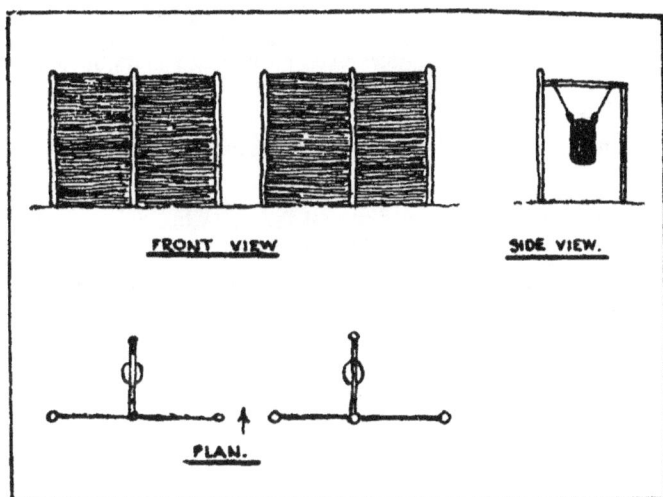

FIG. 20.

The next obstacle could be so arranged that only one or two men in the detail will have to surmount it, the others having a clear way before them.

Fig. 20 illustrates a suggestion for a one-man obstacle. It consists of two screens with a gap about two feet wide between them. Behind each screen, concealed from the view of an approaching man, is fixed a hanging dummy sack. This obstacle presents no physical difficulty, but a problem to the man who on passing through the gap between the screens is suddenly confronted by two opponents, one on his left, the other on his right. The hanging dummy could, of course, be replaced by prone dummies or one of each could be used.

Between this obstacle and the next other dummies can be placed, some behind natural cover, some in shallow slit trenches or lashed to trees. Do not place them across the course in a line, but stagger them so that some men will be in action against a dummy whilst others are still advancing. Remember, in actual combat an enemy may offer every bit as much of an obstacle to one member of an assault as barbed wire may to another.

41

Our next obstacle could again be one for the entire party, and an arrangement similar to that shown in Fig. 21 is suggested. It consists of three or more poles fixed horizontally and about four feet from the ground, the distance between each horizontal being about two feet.

Dummies are lashed to the last horizontal, offering a target for an imaginary shot and a bayonet thrust from an unusual angle as the men crawl under the obstacle. Another set of prone dummies could be arranged just past the obstacle, so that a quick recovery and a " point " are demanded.

More individual obstacles can now be placed about and then another general one similar to that illustrated in Fig. 22. The purpose of this lay-out is to teach the assault not to " bunch." The obstacle consists of simple barbed-wire fences arranged as shown, behind which is built a low wall of turf or sandbags. At the rear of the wall dummy sacks are placed on the ground.

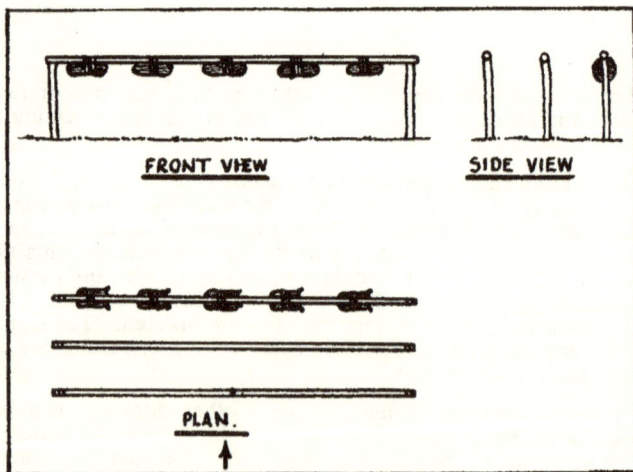

FRONT VIEW   SIDE VIEW

PLAN.

Fig. 21.

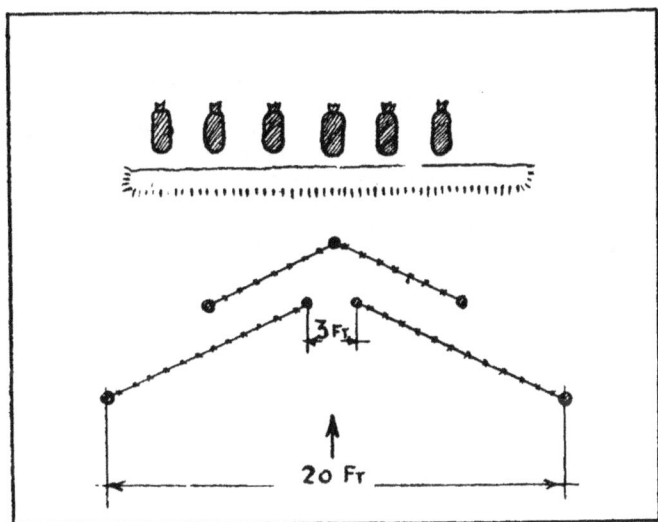

FIG. 22.

The natural tendency of the assault is to converge upon the gap in the wire fences with a resultant bunching and an increase of vulnerability to enemy fire. The assault must learn to surmount this obstacle in line, some passing under or between the wire and just the centre man through the three-foot gap in the fence.

If tommy-gunners are included in the detail their duty will be to cover the bayonet men and keep the heads of the enemy down whilst the obstacle is being traversed. The bayonet men, too, could fire a volley just prior to their effort to pass the obstacle.

It may now be decided to complete the course with a final obstacle representing the enemy position which is the objective of the assault, and it is suggested that an obstacle similar to Fig. 19 is most suitable. This final objective should be sighted in a likely position for an enemy post, just inside a wood on high ground, for example.

Having attained its objective, the assault should not peter out but should advance to a suitable position and consolidate in all-round defence.

This, then, is an example for your consideration. Plan your own course, however, use your ground to its best advantage, and build your obstacles to represent the type of difficulty that, in your own particular locality, you may have to overcome. If you are defending a built-up area, design your obstacles to represent brick walls, doorways, windows in house walls; and any type of local obstacle which you may be faced with in warfare. If you are situated in an area where natural obstacles abound, then design your assault course accordingly. Remember always the golden rule: " Train as you expect and intend to fight."

www.ingramcontent.com/pod-product-compliance
Lightning Source LLC
Chambersburg PA
CBHW020953030426
42339CB00004B/78